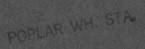

V O Y A G E R

Published by Smart Apple Media

123 South Broad Street

Mankato, Minnesota 56001

Copyright © 2000 Smart Apple Media.

International copyright reserved in all countries. No part

of this book may be reproduced in any form without written

permission from the publisher.

Printed in the United States of America.

Photos: nasa/jpl/caltech

Design and Production: EvansDay Design

Library of Congress Cataloging-in-Publication Data

Hakkila, Jon Eric, 1957–

Voyager / by Jon Hakkila and Adele D. Richardson

p. cm. — (Above and beyond)

Includes index.

Summary: Examines the Voyager spacecraft and their role

in the exploration of outer space.

ISBN 1-58340-053-2

1. Voyager Project—Juvenile literature. [1. Voyager Project.

2. Outer space—Exploration.] I. Richardson, Adele, 1966–.

II. Title. III. Series: Above and beyond (Mankato, Minn.)

TL789.8.U6V5254   1999

523.2—DC21   98-20885

First edition

1 3 5 7 9 8 6 4 2

VOYAGER

DR. JON HAKKILA & ADELE D. RICHARDSON

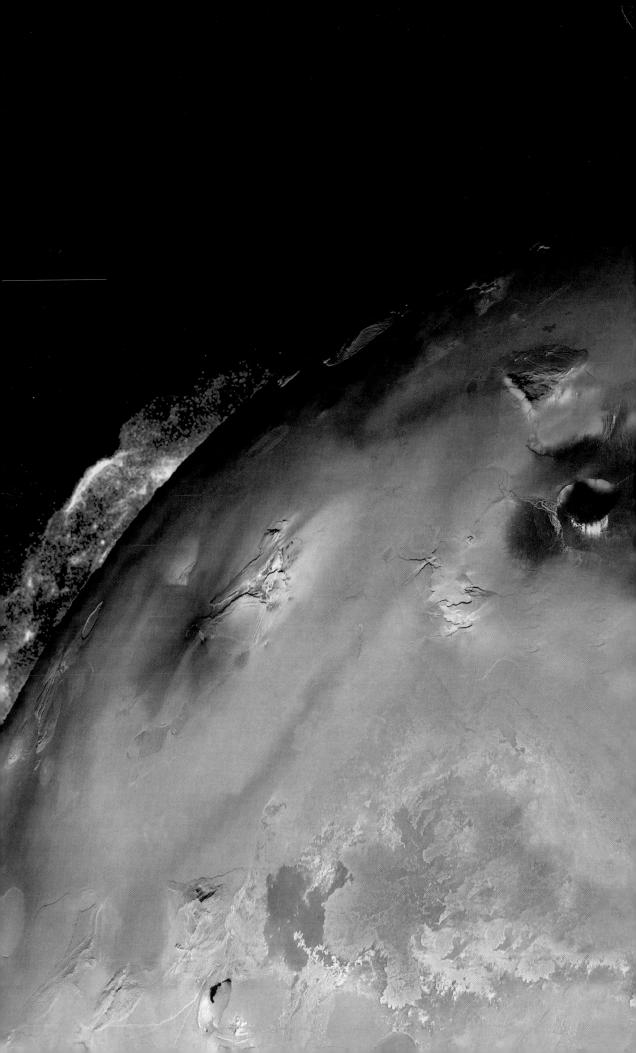

ON OCTOBER 2, 1989, as *Voyager 2* prepared to end its exploration of Neptune, it took one last look at Triton, one of the planet's more interesting moons ✳ Suddenly, an icy volcano erupted violently, spewing dark material nearly five miles (8 km) up from the surface ✳ Astronomers and scientists back on Earth were amazed ✳ Not only did Triton have a thin atmosphere, but it also had active volcanoes, which meant that it could be more than just a dead moon—it could possibly be a small planet trapped in Neptune's gravity ✳ As scientists pored over the new discovery, *Voyager 2* turned away from the planet and its moon, heading into the inky blackness of deep space ✳

Countdown to Voyager

For hundreds of years, the planets in our **solar system** were studied through telescopes. This method of exploration led to a wealth of information, including the discovery of new planets. But scientists knew that they could learn only so much about a planet by watching it from millions, if not billions, of miles away. To truly explore these distant planets, scientists would have to see them up close. To send exploratory equipment that far into space, however, would require advanced rocket technology.

On October 4, 1957, the Soviet Union launched *Sputnik 1*, the world's first **satellite**, into orbit. A few months later, in January 1958, the United States also launched its first satellite, *Explorer 1*. This launch signaled the beginning of a new and exciting space program. Soon, more satellites were launched, then animals and men were sent into orbit. The National Aeronautics and Space Administration (NASA) was created on October 1, 1958, to oversee America's space program. By the mid-1960s, **space probes** were sent to explore Earth's moon and planetary neighbors: Mercury, Venus, and Mars. In July 1969, Americans successfully landed on the moon, making the U.S. a leader in space exploration, a title it has maintained since.

The first attempts to explore the outer planets were through the *Pioneer 10* and *Pioneer 11* spacecraft, launched in 1972 and 1973. Their successful missions to photograph and study the planets Jupiter and Saturn encouraged NASA to continue developing space exploration vehicles. The success of the *Pioneer* program was extremely important;

Much of our knowledge of Saturn has been gained through the Voyager *explorers.*

A **solar system** *is a star and the celestial bodies that orbit it.*

A **satellite** *is an object— natural or man-made—that orbits a celestial body.*

A **space probe** *is a small spacecraft designed to study planets or moons.*

if the missions had failed, the *Voyager* spacecraft may have never been completed. Today, these *Pioneer* explorers are still heading toward deep space.

While the *Pioneer* spacecraft were being developed and launched, scientists at the Jet Propulsion Laboratory—a branch of NASA—in California came to an interesting realization. In the late 1970s, the outer planets of our solar system would be positioned in a unique spiral pattern that happens only once every 175 years. Scientists quickly began developing a plan to build a spacecraft to explore four of the five outer planets.

Because its path of travel would take the spacecraft far from the sun, it wouldn't be able to use the sun's energy for power. Instead, nuclear power would be used, along with "gravity assists" from other planets. The special alignment of the planets made these gravity assists possible. As the spacecraft neared one planet, it would be caught in the planet's gravity and increase in speed as it flew closer to the surface. As it curved around the planet, its momentum would fling it toward the next one.

In 1972, the U.S. government approved money for the building of the *Voyager* spacecraft. In the end, NASA had two spacecraft built; one was to be a backup in case the

A rare alignment of our solar system's outer planets made the Voyager journeys possible.

first one was damaged and couldn't continue the mission. The *Voyager* spacecraft were both designed and built at the Jet Propulsion Laboratory with the help of astronomers, engineers, mathematicians, and more than 150 scientists from around the world.

Carl Sagan, a prominent scientist known for his research on the possibility of extraterrestrial life, selected a variety of pictures and recordings that each spacecraft would carry in case one of the two met up with intelligent life in space. These recordings, which were placed on a phonograph record, included sounds of nature, a baby crying, a human heartbeat, and greetings in 55 different languages.

Voyager 2 was launched from Cape Canaveral, Florida, on August 20, 1977. *Voyager 1* took off more than two weeks later on September 5, 1977, but would reach Jupiter first because of its different **trajectory**.

The "Sounds of Earth" recordings carried by both spacecraft.

The Voyager spacecraft were carried from Earth by powerful Titan-Centaur rockets.

A **trajectory** is the flight path of an object in space.

Tools of Exploration

Voyager 1 and Voyager 2 are identical spacecraft. Each weighed about 1,800 pounds (810 kg) at launch and carry instruments to conduct 11 different types of scientific investigations. The outer design of the spacecraft makes them look rather awkward. Each has a 10-sided drum base measuring six feet (2 m) across with a bowl-shaped antenna on top and heavy equipment and antennas sticking out in several directions.

The dish antennas on top of the Voyager spacecraft measure 12 feet (3.6 m) across. These dishes enable the spacecraft to send information back to Earth and to receive commands from scientists. The radio on board each vehicle has also been useful in studying the outer planets' atmospheres and gravity with invisible radio waves.

Other types of exploration are carried out with optical instruments. These instruments are mounted on an arm that juts out from one side of the spacecraft. Two of the instruments are cameras: a wide angle camera for taking large pictures, and a narrow angle camera for close-up shots. The narrow angle camera is so powerful that it can read the fine print on a newspaper at a distance of more than half a mile (1 km).

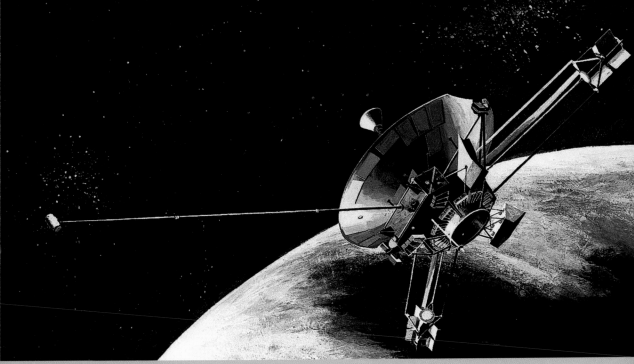

An important part of each Voyager's mission was the study of our solar system's many moons.

Under the cameras is a **photopolarimeter**. This is a type of small telescope that uses light to study substances in a planet's atmosphere and to determine their composition, or what they are made of. Nearby are two **spectrometers**, which are also types of telescopes. Spectrometers separate light into the band, or rainbow of colors, of which it is made. These colors can indicate not only an object's composition, but also its temperature.

A **spectrometer** *is an instrument used to identify substances by studying the distribution of atoms or molecules.*

A **photopolarimeter** *(foh-toh-poh-luh-RIM-et-er) is a telescope that studies the properties of light.*

Other instruments on board the *Voyager* spacecraft are used to measure the particles emitted by the sun (called solar wind), the materials an object contains, **plasma**, and a planet's **magnetic field**. A long arm that reaches far from the spacecraft is called a magnetometer, one of the instruments used to study magnetic fields. Two smaller antennas that form a *V* under the magnetometer are used to examine the plasma in a planet's gas-filled atmosphere.

In addition to this array of instruments, there are six computers on board that process all of the information sent to and from Earth. Each spacecraft also has a digital tape recorder, allowing it to record information for later transmission back to Earth. These recorders have proven to be amazingly reliable; neither the tape nor the recorder has ever developed a problem. The information gathered

Plasma *are charged particles in a gaseous atmosphere that can conduct electricity.*

A planet's **magnetic field** *is the surrounding space that attracts objects.*

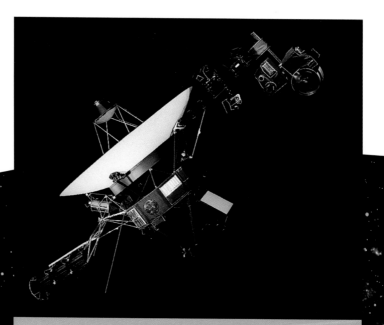

Each Voyager *performed well beyond the expectations of scientists.*

by the *Voyager* spacecraft is sent to the Deep Space Network at the Jet Propulsion Laboratory. Once the data has been processed, it is made available to scientists throughout the U.S. for study.

The *Voyager* spacecraft are powered by plutonium, a nuclear fuel. As the fuel breaks down, it produces heat, which is changed into electricity to power the instruments. To adjust the course of the spacecraft, small rockets attached to the drum part of each vehicle are controlled from Earth. Because of the gravity assists used by the spacecraft, there was no need for a lot of heavy rockets and fuel. In fact, the *Voyager* spacecraft are extremely fuel-efficient. When *Voyager 2* approached Neptune in 1989, it was averaging 30,000 miles (50,000 km) for every gallon of fuel.

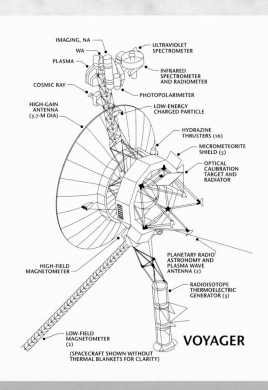

IMAGING, NA
WA
ULTRAVIOLET SPECTROMETER
PLASMA
INFRARED SPECTROMETER AND RADIOMETER
COSMIC RAY
PHOTOPOLARIMETER
HIGH-GAIN ANTENNA (3.7-M DIA)
LOW-ENERGY CHARGED PARTICLE
HYDRAZINE THRUSTERS (16)
MICROMETEORITE SHIELD (5)
OPTICAL CALIBRATION TARGET AND RADIATOR
PLANETARY RADIO ASTRONOMY AND PLASMA WAVE ANTENNA (2)
HIGH-FIELD MAGNETOMETER
RADIOISOTOPE THERMOELECTRIC GENERATOR (3)
LOW-FIELD MAGNETOMETER (2)
VOYAGER
(SPACECRAFT SHOWN WITHOUT THERMAL BLANKETS FOR CLARITY)

A drawing depicting the structure of the exploratory spacecraft.

Giants in Space

The first destination of the *Voyager* explorers was Jupiter, the largest planet in our solar system. *Voyager 1* arrived first on March 5, 1979, four months before *Voyager 2*. Its arrival, however, was a rocky one—*Voyager 1* flew by too close to the planet and was attacked by large amounts of radiation that damaged some of the equipment on board. To prevent this from happening again, scientists adjusted *Voyager 2*'s course to keep it farther from the planet.

In addition to sending more than 33,000 photographs back for scientists to study, the spacecraft made some exciting discoveries about Jupiter. They found that the big planet is made up mostly of the gases hydrogen and helium, and that the center of the planet is nearly five times hotter than the sun. As *Voyager 1* traveled on the dark side of Jupiter, it found an atmosphere crackling with lightning storms and huge **auroras** thousands of miles wide. The colorful bands that can be seen across the planet are caused by fierce winds blowing through the atmosphere, and the white patches that can be seen in many pictures are giant blizzards in which **ammonia** falls like snow.

The *Voyager* spacecraft also discovered that Jupiter has a ring. This ring, however, is so small that it was never

The swirling spots in Jupiter's atmosphere are huge, violent storms, some of which are decades old.

Auroras *are streams or arches of light that glow in a night sky.*

Ammonia *is a colorless gas; cold temperature and pressure can turn it to liquid.*

seen from Earth through a telescope. At its widest point, it is only half a mile (1 km) thick.

The spacecraft also explored the four moons of Jupiter. Scientists were surprised to learn that the moon Io had eight active volcanoes that were shooting debris up to 100 miles (161 km) from the surface. The moon Europa was found to be covered with a thin layer of ice and slush. Callisto and Ganymede, the other two moons, revealed surfaces dotted with craters, indicating that asteroids or comets may have smashed into them at one time.

Once the *Voyager* spacecraft finished their exploration of Jupiter, they raced toward the next planet, Saturn, covering more than 600,000 miles (966,000 km) a day.

Voyager 1 was the first to arrive at Saturn, our solar system's second largest planet, on November 11, 1980; *Voyager 2* didn't arrive until August 25, 1981. As the spacecraft began examining the ringed planet, many new discoveries were sent back to Earth. Before the explorers reached Saturn, astronomers and scientists had believed that the planet had only three large rings encircling it. But as the photographs sent from the spacecraft proved, there are

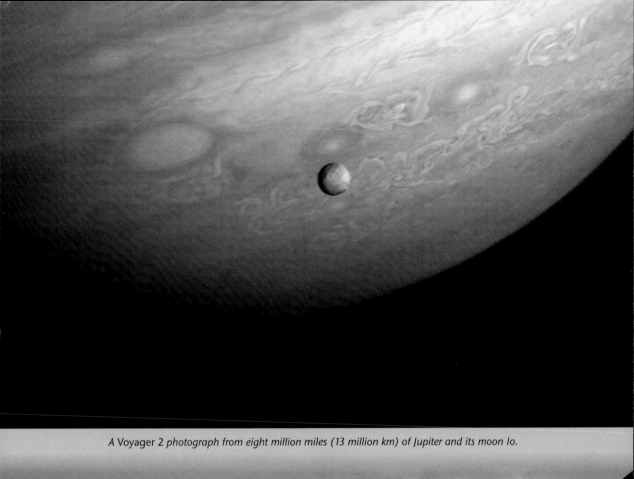

A Voyager 2 photograph from eight million miles (13 million km) of Jupiter and its moon Io.

The Voyager explorers uncovered many of Saturn's secrets.

actually thousands of tiny rings made up of particles of ice, ammonia, rock, and dust. The widest of these rings is only about three miles (5 km) thick.

The *Voyager* spacecraft also discovered that Saturn is extremely light for its size. In fact, if it could be placed in a large enough body of water, Saturn would float. Its atmosphere, like that of Jupiter, churns with lightning and powerful storms. During the *Voyagers'* visit, a huge ammonia hurricane the size of the continent of Asia was spotted. The spacecraft also watched as patches of clouds moved across the planet at more than 2,000 miles (3,220 km) per hour.

Saturn has more moons than any other planet in our solar system. Before the *Voyager* spacecraft arrived, scien-

Two of Saturn's moons: Tethys (top) and Dione.

A Voyager 1 *image of an erupting volcano on the cratered surface of Io.*

tists knew of 10 moons. Information sent back by the spacecraft soon revealed 11 more. Most of these moons are small and dotted with craters, and some have mountains or massive icebergs. Titan, the largest of Saturn's moons, has its own atmosphere; it is one of only two moons in our solar system with this feature.

Once *Voyager 1* finished its exploration, its mission was over. It then left Saturn and headed toward the end of our solar system. Pleased with the success of the completed mission, the U.S. government granted NASA more money so that *Voyager 2* could go on to explore the planet Uranus.

Earth's Distant Neighbors

V*oyager 2*'s instruments first looked at Uranus on November 4, 1985. It would take more than two additional months, however, for the spacecraft to reach the closest point—50,000 miles (80,500 km) from the surface—it would ever come to the planet.

Uranus is one of the strangest of the planets in our solar system for one obvious reason: it lays on its side. The north pole constantly faces the sun for 42 years before turning away. Scientists believe that this strange tilt may have been caused by a collision with a comet or other large object many years ago. The planet's atmosphere is filled with a thick, orange-brown smog made up mainly of hydrogen. When seen through a telescope, though, the planet looks blue. Many scientists think that the blue color is caused by the atmosphere's methane gas, which absorbs red light.

Voyager 2 discovered a huge tail of the planet's magnetic field trailing into space for millions of miles in a corkscrew fashion. The spacecraft also found that Uranus' entire southern hemisphere glows, a phenomenon scientists have no explanation for. Like Jupiter and Saturn, Uranus also has rings around it. Telescopes from Earth

A 1986 photograph of the icy blue Uranus from Voyager 2.

had identified nine rings before *Voyager 2* had even begun its mission, but the explorer found two more as it circled the planet.

The moons of Uranus are dark, icy chunks of rock, carbon, and water. Five moons were known to exist before the spacecraft's exploration, but *Voyager 2* discovered 10 more orbiting the planet. Six of these moons are small, black objects, leading some scientists to believe that they may actually be large chunks of material that came from the rings.

Because of the planet's strange tilt, *Voyager 2* did not spend as much time studying Uranus as it had the other planets. The planet's lopsidedness creates a unique magnetic field that offered the spacecraft no resistance as it circled. As a result, *Voyager 2* shot past the planet like a rocket. Its observation of Uranus officially ended on February 25, 1986. The spacecraft then flew toward the last planet it would study: Neptune.

Oberon: the outermost moon of Uranus.

When *Voyager 2* arrived at Neptune on August 25, 1989, it had been traveling for 12 years and had covered more than 4 billion miles (6.4 billion km). As the spacecraft discovered, Neptune's atmosphere is also filled with violent storms and powerful winds that can move up to 1,200 miles (2,000 km) per hour. One storm had formed an area on the southern hemisphere that scientists called the Great Dark Spot. Strangely, this spot had vanished by 1994, when scientists tried to look at it with the *Hubble Space Telescope*, a massive telescope placed into orbit around the earth.

Neptune was known to have two moons before *Voyager*

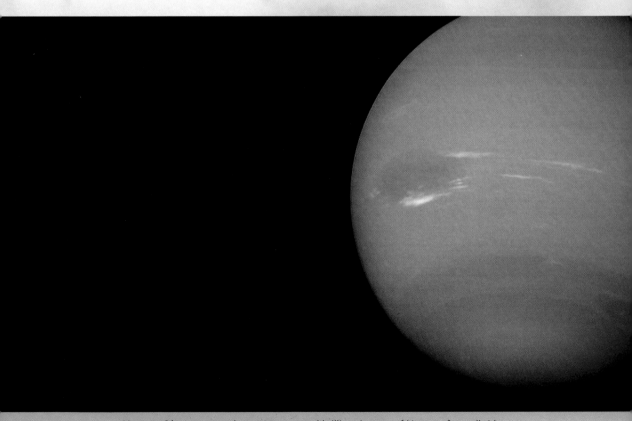

Voyager 2's narrow-angle camera captured brilliant images of Neptune from all sides.

2 arrived, but the spacecraft soon discovered six more. Triton, one of the larger moons, proved to travel in a **retrograde orbit**, or opposite that of other moons. Because of its backward orbit, Triton is slowly falling toward Neptune. Scientists believe that, millions of years from now, the moon will eventually fall far enough that it will be destroyed.

Voyager 2 discovered rings around this planet as well. In 1984, scientists discovered three incomplete ring sections circling Neptune; pictures from *Voyager 2* showed that the sections were all part of one narrow ring. The spacecraft then found three more thin rings spread out around the planet.

Voyager 2's Neptune mission ended on October 2, 1989, when it too headed for the deep space beyond the bounds of our solar system.

*A moon in a **retrograde orbit** circles a planet in a direction opposite from normal.*

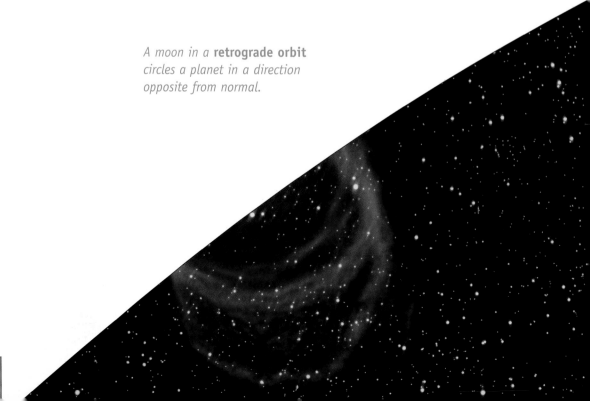

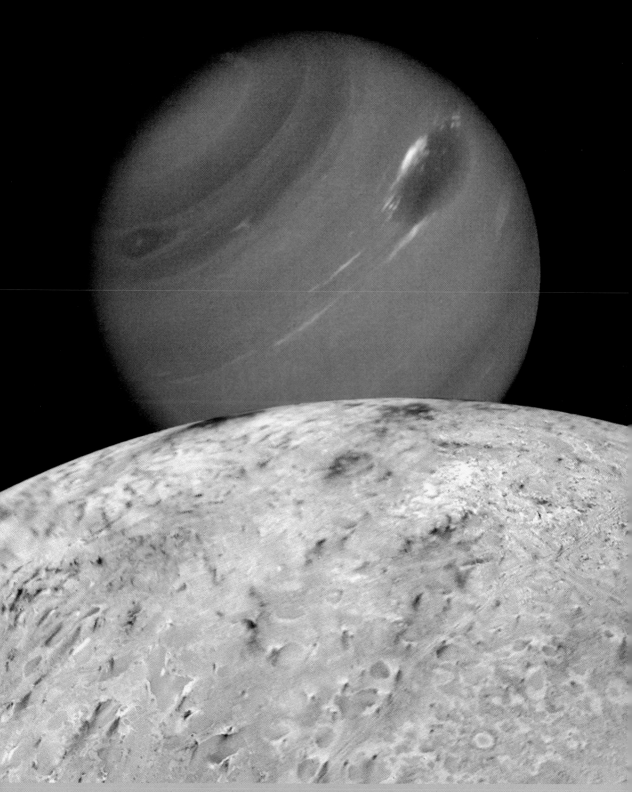

Neptune and its Great Dark Spot loom behind Triton, the distant planet's biggest moon.

Beyond
the Planets

The *Voyager* missions did not stop after *Voyager 2* left Neptune. The spacecraft will continue on past Pluto's line of orbit and through the **heliopause**. *Voyager 1* is expected to reach the inner boundaries of the heliopause in 2001 and exit the other side in 2006, providing it isn't crippled by a collision with space debris.

To conserve the remaining fuel on board the *Voyager* spacecraft, a series of system shut-downs will occur, leaving active only the instruments necessary to continue operation. *Voyager 2*'s shut-down schedule began in 1998 when some of the cameras were turned off. In 2010, the equipment used to steer the spacecraft will no longer operate, and in 2012, its tape recorders will shut down.

Voyager 1's schedule is slightly different. Cameras will be turned off in 2000, tape recorders in 2010, and directional equipment in 2011. By the year 2020, both spacecraft will have run out of energy, shutting down all systems on board.

Our solar system actually extends beyond the heliopause, and the odds are good that neither *Voyager*

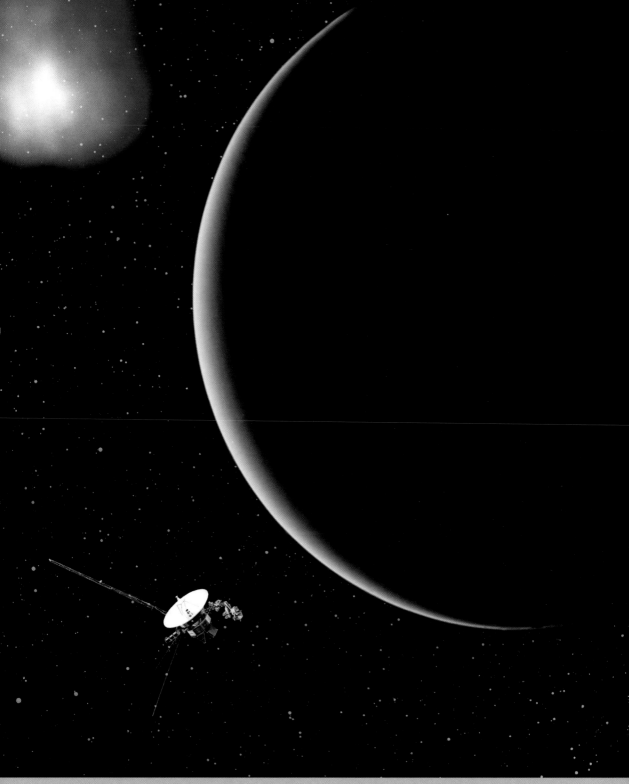

As their equipment is shut down, the Voyager spacecraft will continue to travel toward the edge of our solar system.

The **heliopause** is an invisible boundary where the sun's light ends and deep space begins.

spacecraft will ever leave it. Thousands of times farther out is Oort's Cloud, which is where many comets are believed to originate. Scientists theorize that there may be more than one trillion comets swarming around in the cloud. This fascinating region is so deep into space that even if the *Voyager* spacecraft traveled at a constant speed of 35,000 miles (56,350 km) per hour, it would still take them more than 20,000 Earth years to reach the cloud.

The *Voyager* spacecraft have added a tremendous amount of information to our knowledge of our solar system's planets and moons. By the time *Voyager 2* left Neptune, more than five trillion **bits** of scientific data had been sent back by both vehicles combined. This is enough information to fill more than 6,000 complete sets of the *Encyclopedia Britannica*.

Not only have *Voyager 1* and *Voyager 2* gathered incredible amounts of information about the solar system, but they have also shown us how harsh and violent Earth's neighboring planets can be. Perhaps the *Voyager* explorers' greatest revelation is just how wonderful and unique our own planet really is.

Bits *are the smallest pieces of information a computer can understand.*

Earth: the only known planet able to support life.

INDEX